I have feelings

Bobbie Kalman

Crabtree Publishing Company

www.crabtreebooks.com

Created by Bobbie Kalman

Author and Editor-in-Chief
Bobbie Kalman

Educational consultants
Joan King
Reagan Miller
Elaine Hurst

Editors
Joan King
Reagan Miller
Kathy Middleton

Proofreader
Crystal Sikkens

Design
Bobbie Kalman
Katherine Berti

Photo research
Bobbie Kalman

Production coordinator
Katherine Berti

Prepress technician
Katherine Berti

Photographs by Shutterstock

Library and Archives Canada Cataloguing in Publication

Kalman, Bobbie, 1947-
     I have feelings / Bobbie Kalman.

(My world)
ISBN 978-0-7787-9417-2 (bound).--ISBN 978-0-7787-9461-5 (pbk.)

     1. Emotions--Juvenile literature. I. Title.
II. Series: My world (St. Catharines, Ont.)

BF561.K34 2010   j152.4   C2009-906052-3

Library of Congress Cataloging-in-Publication Data

Available at Library of Congress

Crabtree Publishing Company

Printed in China/122009/CT20091009

www.crabtreebooks.com   1-800-387-7650

Published in Canada
Crabtree Publishing
616 Welland Ave.
St. Catharines, Ontario
L2M 5V6

Published in the United States
Crabtree Publishing
PMB 59051
350 Fifth Avenue, 59th Floor
New York, New York 10118

Published in the United Kingdom
Crabtree Publishing
Maritime House
Basin Road North, Hove
BN41 1WR

Published in Australia
Crabtree Publishing
386 Mt. Alexander Rd.
Ascot Vale (Melbourne)
VIC 3032

Words to know

angry
mad   brave   happy   proud

sad   scared   silly

I am feeling happy.

I am feeling sad.

I am feeling angry.

I am feeling mad.

I am feeling scared.

I am feeling brave.

I am feeling silly.

I am feeling proud.

I like these feelings.

happy   brave   proud   silly

I do not like these feelings.

sad   mad   angry   scared

Activity

Do you have these feelings?

surprised

confused

smart

excited

ashamed

joyful

beautiful

great

wonderful

amazing

glad

confident

15

Notes for adults

Talking about feelings
This book introduces children to the feelings they might like or dislike. Ask them to describe how it feels to be happy, sad, mad, proud, silly, confident, confused, ashamed, or excited. Have them name some events that trigger certain feelings or emotions. Talking about feelings is a good way to understand that feelings, whether they make us feel good or bad, are normal.

Act it out!
Write the vocabulary words about feelings introduced in the book on index cards. Write one feeling on each card. Lay the cards face down. Have children take turns picking a card and then acting out the emotion using facial expressions, body language, and actions. The other children can guess which emotion the student is showing. The pictures in this book will make them aware of some facial expressions and body language that correspond with certain feelings.

Color your feelings
Show some sheets of colored paper to your students. Ask them to describe their feelings when they see each of the colors. Does pink make them feel happy and blue make them feel sad? Read out the feelings vocabulary in this book and ask them which color best describes each feeling.